**This
Read, Listen, & Wonder
book belongs to:**

_____

_____

_____

CANDLEWICK PRESS

About Turtles

Sea turtles are related
to tortoises and terrapins.
They are all reptiles.

Sea turtles are great wanderers,
traveling thousands of miles
each year, often far from land.
This makes them difficult to
study. So scientists are only just
beginning to find out about
their mysterious lives.

There are seven species of sea
turtles. This book is about the
loggerhead turtle. Loggerheads
live in seas all over the world.

For Joseph and Gabriel,
Zoe and Finnian
N. D.

For Auntie Sam, our tortoise-sitter
J. C.

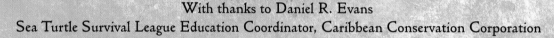

With thanks to Daniel R. Evans
Sea Turtle Survival League Education Coordinator, Caribbean Conservation Corporation

Text copyright © 2001 by Nicola Davies
Illustrations copyright © 2001 by Jane Chapman

First U.S. paperback edition with CD 2008

The Library of Congress has cataloged the hardcover edition as follows:

Davies, Nicola.
One tiny turtle / Nicola Davies ; illustrated by Jane Chapman. —1st U.S. ed.
p.   cm.
ISBN 978-0-7636-1549-9
1. Loggerhead turtle—Juvenile literature.
[1. Loggerhead turtle. 2. Turtles.] I. Chapman, Jane, ill. II. Title.
QL666.C536 D38 2001
597.92'8—dc21   00-052326

ISBN 978-0-7636-2311-1 (paperback)
ISBN 978-0-7636-3834-4 (paperback with CD)

14 15 16 SWT 12 11 10 9 8 7 6 5

Printed in Dongguan, Guangdong, China

This book was typeset in Goldentype.
The illustrations were done in acrylic.

Candlewick Press
99 Dover Street
Somerville, Massachusetts 02144

visit us at www.candlewick.com

One Tiny
TURTLE

Nicola Davies

illustrated by Jane Chapman

CANDLEWICK PRESS

Far, far out to sea,
land is only a memory, and
empty sky touches the water.

Just beneath the surface
is a tangle of weed and driftwood
where tiny creatures cling.
This is the nursery of a sea turtle.

Passing in a boat,
you might not notice the turtle.
Not much bigger than a bottle top,
she hides in the green shadows.

She's a baby, so her shell is soft as old leather.
Just a little fish bite could rip it open.
But the turtle is safe in her world of weed
and snaps her beak on tiny crabs
and shrimps.

Turtles have shells that cover their backs and shells that cover their stomachs. The shells are made from bony plates that get bigger and harder as the turtle grows.

The turtle swims
around, flapping her long front flippers
like wings. She is flying underwater.

She pokes her pinprick nostrils
through the silver surface
to take a quick breath, so fast,
blink and you'd miss it!

Fish breathe underwater, but turtles are reptiles
and need to come up to the surface for air.
They do this every four to five minutes when they are active.
When they are asleep, they can stay underwater for hours.

Then she's gone,
diving down into
her secret life again.

11

For three or four years, maybe more, the turtle rides out the storms

and floats through
the hot calms.

Steadily she outgrows her nursery.

Nobody sees her leave,
but when you look for her,
she has vanished all the same.

A year or two later she turns up close to land.
Bigger than a dinner plate now,
she's not a fish snack anymore.
Her shell is hard as armor.
Her head is tough as a helmet.
She's grown into her name: Loggerhead.

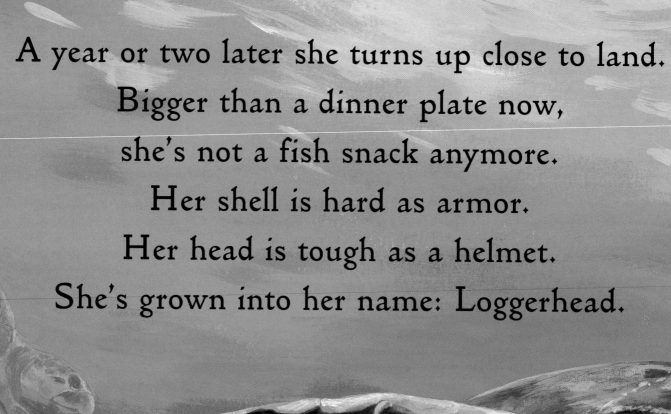

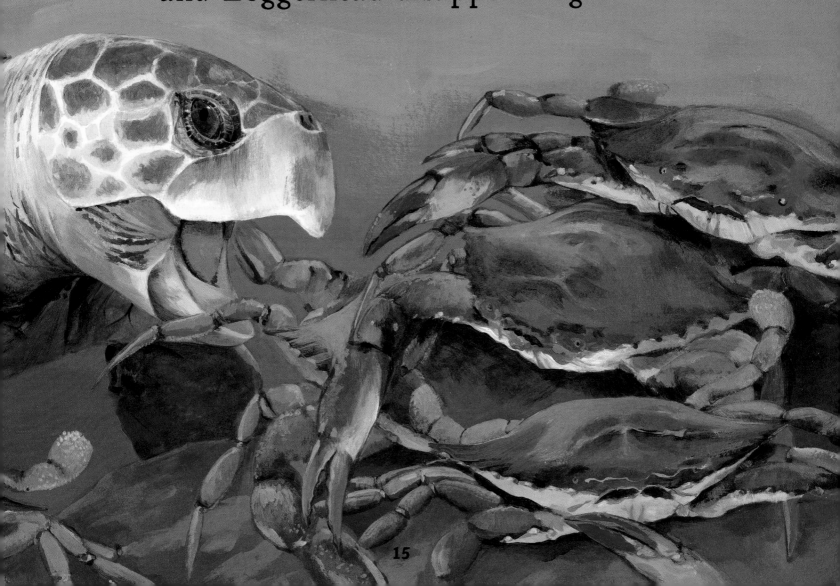

She has come to eat crabs.
Millions swim up from deep water
to breed in the shallows.
Their shells crack as easily as
hens' eggs in her heavy jaws.
But in a week the feast is over
and Loggerhead disappears again.

Loggerhead wanders far and wide
in search of food.

In summer to cool seaweed jungles, where
she finds juicy clams and shoals of shrimps.

And in winter to turquoise lagoons, warm as
a bath, where she can munch among corals.

Loggerhead may travel thousands of miles, but
she leaves no trace or track for you to follow.
Only good luck will catch you a glimpse of her.

For thirty years you might not find her.
Then one summer night she arrives,
on the beach where she was born.
She's found her way here, sensing north
and south like a compass needle, feeling
the current and the warmth of the waves.
She remembers the taste of the water
here and the sound of the surf.

Male turtles wait just off the nesting beaches.

They mate with the females.

Then the females come ashore to lay eggs.

Loggerhead has grown in her wandering years.
She's big as a barrel now.
Floating in the sea she weighs nothing,
but on land she's heavier than a man.
So every flipper step is a struggle,
and her eyes stream with salty tears,
which help keep them free of sand.

Coming ashore is very risky for sea turtles—they can easily overheat and die. So they only nest at night or in cool weather. Then they get back to the sea as soon as possible.

Loggerhead makes
her nest where the
sea won't reach.

Scooping carefully with
her hind flippers . . .

she makes a steep deep hole.

Inside she lays her eggs,
like a hundred squidgy Ping-Pong balls.

Afterward she covers them with sand
to hide her nest from hungry mouths.

Then Loggerhead is gone again,
back to her secret life.

Left behind, under the sand, her eggs stay
deep and safe. Baby turtles grow inside.

Females stay close to their nesting beach for several months.
In that time they usually make at least four nests,
and sometimes as many as ten.

And before
the summer's over
they wriggle from
their shells.

Turtle eggs in warm sand can be ready to hatch in six weeks. If the sand is cool, they can take three weeks longer.

Above them on the beach a hundred eyes watch,
on the lookout for a meal.
So the hatchlings wait until night.

The horizon, where the sea meets the sky, tells baby turtles which way to turn to get to the water. But street lights and buildings next to the beach can confuse them and make them go the wrong way.

Then they burst through the sand and skitter toward the sea.

27

In the dark, claws and beaks
and grabbing paws
miss only one young turtle.
One day, she'll remember this beach
and come back.

But now she dives under the waves and swims.
Swims and swims!
Out into the arms of the ocean.
Far, far out to sea, land becomes a memory
waiting to wake in the head of the little turtle.

INDEX

Look up the pages
to find out about all
of these turtle things.
Don't forget to look at
both kinds of word –

this kind

and this kind.